Book 1
Quality Assurance
By Solis Tech

&

Book 2
Cryptography
By Solis Tech

&

Book 3
Raspberry Pi 2
By Solis Tech

Book 1
Quality Assurance
By Solis Tech

Software Quality Assurance Made Easy!

Quality Assurance: Software Quality Assurance Made Easy!

Table Of Contents

Introduction

I want to thank you and congratulate you for purchasing the book, *"Quality Assurance: Software Quality Assurance Made Easy"*.

This book contains proven steps and strategies on how to implement Software Quality Assurance.

Software quality assurance evolved from the quality assurance in industrial production in the 1940s. With the introduction of computers and the development of applications, it has become an important aspect of software development. In this book, you will learn about the various concepts of software quality assurance and its application in your workplace.

Chapter 1 talks about the definitions of software quality assurance and quality control. It is necessary that you understand what it is so that you can fully grasp the other fundamental concepts. Chapter 2 discusses the ways you can implement software quality assurance in an existing environment. In Chapter 3, you will learn how you can ensure that the software produces quality outputs.

Chapter 4 teaches you how to develop and run software testing while Chapter 5 talks about the timing of the software release. In Chapter 6, you will learn about using automated testing tools.

Thanks again for purchasing this book, I hope you enjoy it!

Chapter 1: **Definition Of Software Quality Assurance And Software Testing**

Software quality assurance is part of the process of software development. It includes the improvement and monitoring of the process. It also follows the processes, procedures, and standards. Furthermore, it ensures the resolution of problems discovered. In effect, it focuses on the prevention of problems.

Software testing, on the other hand, includes the operation of the application or system under controlled conditions, which must include all abnormal and normal conditions. The primary goal of software testing is to know what can go wrong when unexpected and expected scenarios occur. Its focus is on the detection of problems.

Companies differ in assigning responsibilities for quality assurance and software testing. There are organizations that combine both responsibilities to a single person or group. However, it is also common to have various teams that combine developers and testers. Project managers lead such teams. The decision to either combine or separate responsibilities depends on the company's business structure and size. Human beings or machines can perform software testing.

Some projects do not require a group of testers. The need for software testing depends on the project's context and size, the development methodology, the risks, the developers' experience and skill, and other factors. For example, a short-term, low-risk, and small project with expert developers, who know how to use test-first development or thorough unit testing, may not require software test engineers.

In addition, a small or new IT company may not have a dedicated software testing staff even its projects have a need for it. It may outsource software testing or use contractors. It may also adjust its approach on project development and management by using either agile test-first development or more experienced programmers. An inexperienced project manager may use his developers to do their own functional testing or skip thorough testing all together. This decision is highly risky and may cause the project to fail.

If the project is a huge one with non-trivial risks, software testing is important. The use of highly specialized software testers enhances the ability of the project to succeed because different people with different perspectives can offer their invaluable contribution because they have stronger and deeper skills.

In general, a software developer focuses on the technical issues to make a functionality work. On the other hand, a software test engineer focuses on what can go wrong with the functionality. It is very rare to come across a highly effective technical person, who can do both programming and testing tasks. As such, IT companies need software test engineers.

There are various reasons why software may have bugs. First, there is no communication or miscommunication as to the application's requirements. Second, the software is very complex so an inexperienced individual may have a difficult time understanding the software application. In addition, the software may be a big one and includes big databases, data communications, security complexities, different remote and local web services, and multi-tier distributed systems.

Third, there are programming errors. Fourth, the requirements of the software change because the end-user requests for them. In some cases, this end-user may not be aware of the effects of such changes, which can result in errors. The staff's enthusiasm is affected. Continuous modification requirements are a reality. Quality assurance and software test engineers must be able to plan and adapt continuous testing to prevent bugs from affecting the software.

Fifth, time pressures can be difficult to manage. Mistakes often occur during crunch times. Sixth, people involved in the project may not be able to manage their own egos. Seventh, the code has poor documentation or design. It is difficult to modify and maintain codes that are poorly written or documented. Bugs can occur if IT companies do not offer incentives for developers to write maintainable, understandable, and clear codes. Most companies offer incentives when they are able to finish the code quickly. Eighth, the use of software development tools can also result to bugs.

How Quality Assurance Evolved

In 1946, the US Occupation Forces established the Quality Movement in Japan. The movement follows the research of W. Edwards Deming and the Statistical Process Control papers. The methods discussed by the research and papers pertained to industrial production. Each process of production has an output with a required specification and a verifiable main product. The Quality Control group measures the output at different production stages. It ensures that the output falls within the acceptable variances.

The Quality Assurance group does not part in the production process. It audits the process to ensure compliance with the established standards and guidelines. It gives its input for the continuous improvement of the process. In a manufacturing setup, it is easy to differentiate between quality assurance and quality control. These methods become the norm in manufacturing. Since they work in industrial production, they spawned the birth of software quality control and software quality assurance.

Quality Attributes Of Software

Hewlett Packard's Robert Grady developed the common definition of the Software Quality Attributes. The FURPS model identified the following characteristics: functionality, usability, reliability, performance, and supportability (FURPS).

The functional attributes pertain to the features of the software. They answer the question about the purpose of the software instead of its use. The reason for the software's existence is different from the concerns about its reliability, look and feel, and security. The usability attributes are characteristics pertaining to user interface issues like consistency, interface aesthetics, and accessibility.

The reliability attributes include recoverability, accuracy, and availability of the system while performance attributes pertain to issues like startup time, recovery time, system response time, and information throughput. Supportability addresses issues like localizability, scalability, installation, configurability, compatibility, maintainability, adaptability, and testability. The FURPS model evolved into FURPS+ to include specification of constraints like physical, interface, implementation, and design constraints.

The Software Quality Control team tests the quality characteristics. The tests for usability and functionality occur during execution of the actual software. On the other hand, adaptability and supportability tests occur through code inspection. It is not the responsibility of the Software Quality Control or Software Quality Assurance to put the quality attributes into the software. The Software Quality Control team tests for the absence or presence of such characteristics while the Software Quality Assurance group ensures that each stakeholder follow the right standards and procedures during software execution.

In theory, the implementation of FURPS+ will overcome the problems caused by the software's intangible nature because the Software Quality Control team can measure each software attribute. For example, the amount of time it takes for programmers to fix a bug is a measure of supportability. To improve it requires the implementation of new coding standards.

The Software Quality Control group can inspect the code to ensure compliance with the coding standard while the Software Quality Assurance team can ensure that the quality control and programmer teams follow the right standards and process. It is the duty of the Software Quality Assurance group to collect and analyze the time spent on fixing the bug so that it can provide an input in terms of its usefulness to the process improvement initiative.

Chapter 2: Introducing Software Quality Assurance Procedures To An Existing Company

The introduction of the software quality assurance procedures rely on the risks involved and the company's size. If the organization is large and the projects are high-risk, the management must consider a more formal quality assurance process. On the other hand, if the risk is lower, the implementation of quality assurance may be a step-at-a-time procedure. The processes of quality assurance maintain balance with productivity.

If the project or the company is small, an ad-hoc process may be more appropriate. The success of the software development relies on the team leaders and developers. More importantly, there must be enough communications between software testers, managers, customers, and developers. Requirement specifications must be complete, testable, and clear. There must be procedures for design and code reviews, as well as retrospectives. Common approaches used are Agile, Kaizen, and Deming-Shewhart Plan-Do-Check-Act methods.

It is important to evaluate documents, code, specifications, plans, and requirements. To do this, it is necessary to prepare issues lists, checklists, inspection meetings, and walkthroughs. This process is what IT people refer to as verification. On the other hand, validation occurs after verification and includes actual testing of the application. A walkthrough is evaluation in an informal meeting. There is no need to prepare for it.

An inspection is more formal than a walkthrough and attended by at most eight people including a reader, a recorder, and a moderator. Usually, an inspection's subject is a test plan or requirements specification so that the attendees will know the software's problems. The attendees must read the document before attending an inspection so they will find the problems prior to the meeting. It is difficult to prepare for an inspection but it is an effective and least costly way to ensure quality.

Testing Requirements That Must Be Considered

The basis of black box testing is the software's functionality and requirements. A software tester need not be knowledgeable of code or internal design. White box testing, on the other hand, requires knowledge of code. It takes into consideration the code statements, paths, branches, and conditions. Unit testing requires testing of particular code modules or functions. Usually, the application developer performs it because it requires detailed knowledge of the code and program design.

API testing is testing of data exchange or messaging among systems parts. An incremental integration testing tests the application when there is a new functionality, which must be independent to work separately before it can be included in the application. The application programmer or software tester performs this type of testing. An integration testing requires the testing of the various parts of the software in order to know if they work together properly. Functional testing, on the other hand, is a kind of black box testing that focuses on the application's functional requirements. The software testers perform it.

System testing is also another type of black box testing. It includes testing of the general requirements specifications and all the various parts of the software. End-to-end testing, on the other hand, is a macro type of system testing. It includes testing the whole software in various situations that replicates real-world use. Smoke testing or sanity testing is an initial testing to know if the new version is performing well so that major testing can commence. Regression testing retests the application after some modifications or fixes.

Acceptance testing is final testing the software based on customer's specifications. Load testing is software testing under heavy loads in order to find out when the response time of the system fails or degrades. Stress testing, on the other hand, is system functional testing with unusually heavy loads, large complex queries of the database, using large numerical values, and heavy repetition of certain inputs or actions. Performance testing is testing using test or quality assurance plans.

The goal of usability testing depends on the customer or end-user. It uses techniques like surveys, user interviews, and user sessions' video recording. Software testers and developers are not the people to implement usability testing. Install/uninstall testing uses processes to test upgrade, full, or partial install/uninstall of the software. Recovery testing determines how the software can recover in catastrophic instances like hardware failures and crashes. Failover testing is another name for recovery testing.

Security testing tests how the application protects against willful damage, unauthorized access, and the likes. It uses sophisticated testing methods. Compatibility testing tests how the application performs in some environments. Exploratory testing, on the other hand, is an informal and creative testing that does not use any formal test cases or plans. Usually, software testers are new to the application. Ad-hoc testing is almost the same as exploratory testing but the software testers understand the application prior to testing.

Context-driven testing focuses on the software's intended use, culture, and environment. For example, medical equipment software has a different testing approach than a computer game. User acceptance testing determines if the application is satisfactory to the customer or end-user. Comparison testing, on the other hand, compares the software with its competitors.

Alpha testing occurs when the software is almost finished. Usually, end users perform this type of testing. Beta testing is testing when the software is finished and ready for final release. Like alpha testing, this kind of testing is for end users. Finally, mutation testing uses test cases and allows for code changes and retesting using the original test cases to discover software bugs.

Common Problems And Solutions In Developing Software

Software development can encounter common problems like poor user stories or requirements, unrealistic schedule, inadequate testing, featuritis, and miscommunication. Problems can arise if there requirements are incomplete, unclear, not testable, or too general. Furthermore, if the software development has a short timetable, problems can also be evident. If the software does not pass through the testing process, the IT organization will only know of problems if the system crashes or the end users complain.

In addition, problems can arise if the users or customers request for more new functionalities even after the development goals are set. Finally, if there is miscommunication between the programmers and customers, problems are inevitable. If it is an agile project, the problems become evident when it strays away from agile principles.

If there are common problem then there are also common solutions like solid requirements, realistic schedules, adequate testing, sticking to original requirements, and communication. Software requirements must be complete, clear, cohesive, detailed, testable, and attainable. All players concerned must agree upon them. In agile environments, there must be close coordination with end users or customers so that any change in requirement is clear. There must be enough time for design, planning, bug fixing, testing, changes, retesting, and documentation. Each person must not feel burnout during the project.

For testing to be adequate, it must start early. Retesting must occur after each change or fix. There must be enough time for bug fixing and testing. If the end user or customer requests for excessive changes when development has begun, it is important that the project manager explain the consequences. If the change is important, a schedule change is inevitable to accommodate it.

The project manager must manage the expectations of the end users or customer. In an agile environment, the project manager can expect significant change in the initial requirements. There must be a schedule for inspections and walkthroughs. The use of communication tools is important to ensure cooperation and teamwork.

Software Quality Assurance And Software Quality Control In The Workplace

If there is no formal implementation of Software Quality Assurance/Software Quality Control, the quality group can mirror that of an engineering services group. It performs the tasks not done by the development team. It reports to the application development manager. Under this scenario, the manager can instruct the quality assurance personnel to install a load-testing tool and declare him as a performance expert. Although the quality assurance person must perform load testing, it is the job of the software designer/programmer. As such, the software quality assurance/software quality control must be separate from the development team.

Software quality assurance requires the establishment of templates used during reviews. Such templates must have sections for both non-functional and functional requirements. For example, the requirements for performance must be in terms of transaction rates and user population. The use of Traceability Matrix can help in the requirements management. The matrix also encourages the analyst to use individual requirements for cross-referencing.

Software quality assurance verifies that the requirements comply with the templates and that they are not ambiguous. It reviews the risks of non-completion of the non-functional attributes, as well as the Traceability Matrix, to ensure usability of all requirements in other specifications. Software quality assurance can write the test cases, which refer to some of the requirements. It can cross-reference the requirements in the Traceability Matrix.

The interface specification is a requirement if the software is component-based. Software quality assurance must subject the document to verification. It must also subject other lower level specifications to quality assurance if such requirements are critical. Even if there are limited resources for software quality assurance, an IT organization can obtain a good return-on-investment if it pays attention to requirements and interfaces.

Chapter 3: Ensuring Software Quality

Software quality is the delivery of bug-free software within budget and on time. Because quality is subjective, it depends on the customer and his overall influence in the project. A customer can be an end user, a customer contract officer, a customer acceptance tester, a customer manager, a software maintenance engineer, and others. Each customer has his own definition of quality.

A code is good if it works, is secure, bug free, maintainable, and readable. Some companies have standards, which their programmers follow. However, each developer has his own idea about what is best. Standards have different metrics and theories. If there are excessive rules and standards, they can limit creativity and productivity. A design can be functional or internal design.

An internal design is good if the overall structure of the software code is clear, easily modifiable, understandable, and maintainable. It is robust with the capability to log status and with sufficient error handling. Furthermore, the software works as expected. A functional design is good if the software functionality comes from the requirements of the end user and customer. Even an inexperienced user can use the software without reading the user manual or seeking online help.

The software life cycle starts with the conception of the application and commences when the software is no longer used. It includes factors like requirements analysis, initial concept, internal design, functional design, test planning, documentation planning, document preparation, coding, maintenance, testing, integration, retesting, updates, and phase out.

A good software test engineer must possess a test to break attitude, which means that he must be able to focus on the detail in order to ensure that the application is of good quality. He must be diplomatic and tactful so that he can maintain a good relationship with the programmers, the customers, and the managements.

It is helpful if he has previous experience on software development so that he understands the whole process deeply. A good software test engineer is able to appreciate the point of view of the programmers. He must have good judgment skills to be able to determine critical or high-risk application areas that require testing.

A good quality assurance engineer also shares the same qualities with a good software test engineer. Furthermore, he must understand the whole process of software development and the organizations' goals and business approach. He must possess understanding of all sides of issues in order to communicate effectively with everyone concerned. He must be diplomatic and patient, especially in the early stages of the quality assurance process. Lastly, he must be able to detect problems during inspections and reviews.

Qualities Of A Good Quality Assurance Or Test Manager

A good manager must be familiar with the process of software development and must be enthusiastic and promote positivity in the team. He must be able to increase productivity by promoting teamwork and cooperation between quality assurance, software, and test engineers. If the processes require improvements, he must be diplomatic in ensuring smooth implementation of such changes.

He must be able to withstand pressure and offer the right feedback about quality issues to the other managers. He must be able to hire and keep the right personnel. He must possess strong communication skills to deal with everyone concerned in the process. Lastly, he must stay focused and be able to hold meetings.

Importance Of Documentation In Quality Assurance

If the team is large, it is more useful to have the proper documentation for efficient communication and management of projects. Documentation of quality assurance practices is necessary for repeatability. Designs, specifications, configurations, business rules, test plans, code changes, bug reports, test cases, and user manuals must have proper documentation. A system of documentation is necessary for easy obtaining and finding of information.

Each project has its own requirements. If it is an agile project, the requirements may change and evolve. Thus, there is no need for detailed documentation. However, it is useful to document user stories. Documentation on the software requirements describes the functionality and properties of the software. It must be clear, reasonably detailed, complete, attainable, cohesive, and testable. It may be difficult to organize and determine the details but there are tools and methods that are available.

It is important to exercise care in documenting the requirements of the project's customer, who may be an outside or in-house personnel, an end user, a customer contract officer, a customer acceptance tester, a customer manager, a sales person, or a software maintenance engineer. If the project did not meet the expectations, any of these customers can slow down the project.

Each organization has its own way of handling requirements. If the project is an agile project, the requirements are in the user stories. On the other hand, for other projects, the requirements are in the document. Some organizations may use functional specification and high-level project plans. In every requirement, documentation is important to help software testers to make test plans and perform testing. Without any significant documentation, it is impossible to determine if the application meets the user expectations.

Even if the requirements are not testable, it is still important to test the software. The test results must be oriented towards providing information about the risk levels and the status of the application. It is significant to have the correct testing approach to ensure success of the project. In an agile project, various approaches can use methods that require close cooperation and interaction among stakeholders.

Chapter 4: How To Develop And Run Software Testing

To develop the steps for software testing, it is necessary to consider the following.

First, it is important to get the requirements, user stories, internal design, functional design, and any other information that can help with the testing process.

Second, testing must have budget and schedule.

Third, it must have personnel with clear responsibilities.

Fourth, there must be project context to determine testing approaches, scope, and methods.

Fifth, identification of limitations and scope of tests is necessary in order to set priorities.

Sixth, testing must include methods and approaches applicable.

Seventh, it must have the requirements to determine the test environment.

Eighth, it must have requirements for testing tools.

Ninth, it is important to determine the data requirements for testing input.

Tenth, identification of labor requirements and tasks are important.

Eleventh, it must determine milestones, timelines, and schedule estimates.

Twelfth, testing must include error classes, boundary value analysis, and input equivalence classes, when needed.

Thirteenth, it must have a test plan and documents for approvals and reviews.

Fourteenth, testing must determine test scenarios and cases.

Fifteenth, it must include reviews, approvals of test cases, inspections, approaches, and scenarios.

Sixteenth, there must be testing tools and test environment, user manuals, configuration guides, reference documents, installation guides, test tracking processes, archiving and logging processes, and test input data.

Seventeenth, it must include software releases,

The Test Plan

A test plan is a document, which includes scope, objectives, and focus of the software testing activity. To prepare it, it is important to consider the efforts needed to validate the software's acceptability. The test plan must help even those people who are not part of the test group. Testing must be thorough but not very detailed.

The test plan can include the following: the title, the software version number, the plan's revision history, table of contents, the intended audience, the goal of testing, the overview of the software, relevant documents, legal or standards requirements, identifier and naming standards, and requirements for traceability. The test plan must also include overall project organization, test organization, dependencies and assumptions, risk analysis of the project, focus and priorities of testing, limitations and scope, test outline, data input outline, test environment, analysis of test environment validity, configuration and setup of test environment, and processes for software migration among other things.

A test case includes the input, event, or action plus its expected result in order to know if software's functionality is working as planned. It contains test case identifier, objective, test case name, test setup, requirements for input data, steps, and expected results. The details may differ, depending on the project context and organization. Some organizations handle test cases differently. Most of them use less-detailed test scenarios for simplicity and adaptability of test documentation. It is important to develop test cases because it is possible to detect problems and errors in the software through them.

When A Bug Is Discovered

If the software has a bug, the programmers must fix it. The software must undergo retesting after the resolution of the error. Regression testing must be able to check that the solutions performed were not able to create more problems within the application. A system for problem tracking must be set up so it becomes easier to perform the retesting. There are various software tools available to help the quality assurance team.

In tracking the problems, it is good to consider the following: complete information about the bug, bug identifier, present bug status, software version number, how the bug was discovered, specifics about environment and hardware, test case information, bug description, cause of the bug, fix description, retesting results, etc. There must be a reporting process so that the appropriate personnel will know about the errors and fixes.

A configuration management includes the various processes used to coordinate, control, and track requirements, code, problems, documentation, designs, change requests, tools, changes made, and person who made the changes. If the software has many bugs, the software tester must report them and focus on critical bugs. Because this problem can affect the schedule, the software tester must inform the managers and send documentation in order to substantiate the problem.

The decision to stop testing is difficult to do, especially for complex applications. In some cases, complete testing is not possible. Usually, the decision to stop testing considers the deadlines, the degree of test cases completion, the depletion of the test budget, the specified coverage of code, the reduction of the bug rate, and the ending of alpha or beta testing periods. If there is not enough time to perform thorough testing, it is important to focus the testing on important matters based on risk analysis. If the project is small, the testing can depend on risk analysis again.

In some cases, there are organizations that are not serious about quality assurance. For them, it is important to solve problems rather than prevent problems. Problems regarding software quality may not be evident. Furthermore, some organizations reward people who fix problems instead of incentivizing prevention of problems. Risk management includes actions that prevent things from happening. It is a shared responsibility among stakeholders. However, there must be a point person who is primarily responsible for it. In most cases, the responsibility falls on the quality assurance personnel.

Chapter 5: Deciding When To Release The Software To Users

In most projects, the decision to release the software depends on the timing of the end testing. However, for most applications, it is difficult to specify the release criteria without using subjectivity and assumptions. If the basis of the release criteria is the result of a specific test, there is an assumption that this test has addressed all the necessary software risks.

For many projects, this is impossible to do without incurring huge expenses. Therefore, the decision is actually a leap of faith. Furthermore, most projects try to balance cost, timeliness, and quality. As such, testing cannot address the balance of such factors when there is a need to decide on the release date.

Usually, the quality assurance or test manager decides when to release the software. However, this decision involves various assumptions. First, the test manager understands the considerations, which are significant in determining the quality of the software to justify release. Second, the quality of the software may not balance with cost and timeliness. In most organization, there is not enough definition for sufficient quality. Thus, it becomes very subjective and may vary from day to day or project to project.

The release criteria must consider the sales goals, deadlines, market considerations, legal requirements, quality norms of the business segment, programming and technical considerations, expectations of end users, internal budget, impact on the other projects, and a host of other factors. Usually, the project manager must know all these factors.

Because of the various considerations, it may not be possible for the quality assurance manager or test manager to decide the release of the software. However, he may be responsible in providing inputs to the project manager, who makes the release decision. If the project or the organization is small, the decision to release the software rests on the project manager or the product manager. For larger organizations or projects, there must be a committee to decide when to release the software.

If the software requirements change continuously, it is important for all stakeholders to cooperate from the beginning so that they all understand how the change in requirements may affect the project. They may decide on alternate strategies and test plans in advance. It is also beneficial to the project if the initial design of the software can accommodate changes later on. A well-documented code makes it easier for programmers to make the necessary changes.

It is also good to use rapid prototyping if possible so that customers will not make more requests for changes because they are sure of their requirements from the very beginning. The initial schedule of the project must allow extra lead-time for these changes. If possible, all changes must be in the "Phase 2" of the software version. It is important that only easily implemented requirements must be in the project.

The difficult ones must be in the future versions. The management and the customers must know about costs, inherent risks, and scheduling impacts of big changes in the requirements. If they know about the challenges, they can decide whether to continue with the changes or not.

There must be balance between expected efforts with the effort to set up automated testing for the changes. The design of the automated test scripts must be flexible. Its focus must be on aspects of application, which will remain unchanged. The reduction of the appropriate effort for the risk analysis of the changes can be through regression testing.

The design of the test cases must be flexible. The focus must be on ad-hoc testing and not on detailed test cases and test plans. If there is a continuous request for changes in the requirements, it is unreasonable to expect that requirements will remain stable and pre-determined. Thus, it may be appropriate to use approaches for agile development.

It is difficult to determine if software has significant hidden or unexpected functionality. It also indicates that the software development process has deeper problems. The functionality must be removed if does not serve any purpose to the software because it may have unknown dependencies or impacts. If not removed, there must be a consideration for the determination of regression testing needs and risks. The management must know if there are significant risks caused by the unexpected functionality.

The implementation of quality assurance processes is slow over time because the stakeholders must have a consensus. There must be an alignment of processes and organizational goals. As the organization matures, there will be an improvement on productivity. Problem prevention will be the focus. There will be a reduction of burnout and panics. There will be less wasted effort and more improved focus.

The processes must be efficient and simple to prevent any "Process Police" mentality. Furthermore, quality assurance processes promote automated reporting and tracking thereby minimizing paperwork. However, in the short run, implementation may be slow. There will be more days for inspections, reviews, and planning but less time for handling angry end users and late night fixing of errors.

If the growth of the IT organization is very rapid, fixed quality assurance processes may be impossible. Thus, it is important to hire experienced people. The management must prioritize issues about quality and maintain a good relationship with the customers. Every employee must know what quality means to the end user.

Chapter 6: Using Automated Testing Tools

If the project is small, learning and implementing the automated testing tools may not be worth it. However, these automated testing tools are important for large projects. These tools use a standard coding language like Java, ruby, python, or other proprietary scripting language. In some cases, it is necessary to record the first tests for the generation of the test scripts. Automated testing is challenging if there are continuous changes to the software because a change in test code is necessary every time there is a new requirement. In addition, the analysis and interpretation of results can be difficult.

Data driven or keyword driven testing is common in functional testing. The maintenance of actions and data is easy through a spreadsheet. The test drivers read the information for them to perform the required tests. This strategy provides more control, documentation, development, and maintenance of test cases. Automated tools can include code analyzers, coverage analyzers, memory analyzers, load/performance test tools, web test tools, and other tools.

A test engineer, who does manual testing, determines if the application performs as expected. He must be able to judge the expected outcome. However, in an automated test, the computer judges the test outcome. A mechanism must be present for the computer to compare automatically between the actual and expected outcomes for every test scenario. If the test engineer is new to automated testing, it is important that he undergo training first.

Proper planning and analysis are important in selecting and using an automated tool for testing. The right tool must be able to test more thoroughly than manual methods. It must test faster and allow continuous integration. It must also reduce the tedious manual testing. The automation of testing is costly. However, it may be able to provide savings in the long term.

Choosing The Appropriate Test Environment

There is always a tradeoff between cost and test environment. The ultimate scenario is to have a collection of test environments, which mirror exactly all possible usage, data, network, software, and hardware characteristics that the software can use. For most software, it is impossible to predict all environment variations. Furthermore, for complex and large systems, it is extremely expensive to duplicate a live environment.

The reality is that decisions on the software environment characteristics are important. Furthermore, the choice of test environments takes into consideration logistical, budget, and time constraints. People with the most technical experience and knowledge, as well as with the deep understanding of constraints and risks, make these decisions. If the project is low risk or small, it is common to take the informal approach. However, for high risk or large projects, it is important to take a more formalize procedure with many personnel.

It is also possible to coordinate internal testing with efforts for beta testing. In addition, it is possible to create built-in automated tests upon software installation by users. The tests are able to report information through the internet about problems and application environment encountered. Lastly, it is possible to use virtual environments.

The Best Approach To Test Estimation

It is not easy to find the best approach because it depends on the IT organization, the project, as well as the experience of the people involved. If there are two projects with the same size and complexity, the right test effort for life-critical medical software may be very large compared to a project involving an inexpensive computer game. The choice of a test estimation approach based on complexity and size may be applicable to a project but not to the other one.

The implicit risk context approach caters to a quality assurance manager or project manager, who uses risk context with past personal experiences to allocate resources for testing. The risk context assumes that each project is similar to the others. It is an experience-based intuitive guess.

The metrics-based approach, on the other hand, uses past experiences on different projects. If there is already data from a number of projects, the information is beneficial in future test planning. For each new project, the basis of adjustment of required test time is the available metrics. In essence, this is not easy to do because it is judgment based on historical experience.

The test-work breakdown approach decomposes the testing tasks into smaller tasks to estimate testing with a reasonable accuracy. It assumes that the breakdown of testing tasks is predictable and accurate and that it is feasible to estimate the testing effort. If the project is large, this is not feasible because there is a need to extend testing time if there are many bugs. In addition to, there is a need to extend development time.

The iterative approach is for large test projects. An initial rough estimate is necessary prior to testing. Once testing begins and after finishing a small percentage of testing work, there is a need to update the testing estimate because testers have already obtained additional knowledge of the issues, risks, and software quality. There is also a need to update test schedules and plans. After finishing a larger percentage of testing work, the testing estimate requires another update. The cycle continues until testing ends.

The percentage-of-development approach requires a quick way of testing estimation. If the project has 1,000 hours of estimated programming effort, the

IT firm usually assigns a 40% ratio for testing. Therefore, it will allot 400 hours for testing. The usefulness of this approach depends on risk, software type, personnel, and complexity level.

In an agile software development approach, the test estimate is unnecessary if the project uses pure test-driven development although it is common to mix some automated unit tests with either automated or manual functional testing. By the nature of agile-based projects, they are not dependent on testing efforts but on the construction of the software.

Conclusion

Thank you again for purchasing this book!

I hope this book was able to help you to understand the concepts of Software Quality Assurance.

The next step is to apply what you learned from this book to your work.

Finally, if you enjoyed this book, please take the time to share your thoughts and post a review on Amazon. It'd be greatly appreciated!

Thank you and good luck!

Book 2
Cryptography
By Solis Tech

Cryptography Theory & Practice Made Easy!

Cryptography: Cryptography Theory & Practice Made Easy!

Table of Contents

Introduction

I want to thank you and congratulate you for purchasing the book, *Cryptography*.

This book contains tips and techniques on how to build cryptosystems – even if you're just a complete beginner.

This eBook will help you learn about the history and basic principles of cryptography. It will teach you the different aspects of message encryption. In addition, you will learn how to establish cryptosystems. Aside from discussing modern/digital encryption schemes, this book will teach you how to use different types of "practical" ciphers.

Thanks again for purchasing this book. I hope you enjoy it!

Chapter 1: Cryptography – History and Basic Concepts

The Origin of Cryptography

During the ancient times, people needed to do two things: (1) to share information and (2) protect the information they are sharing. These things forced individuals to "encode" their messages. This "encoding" process protects the message in a way that only the intended recipient can understand the information. That means the data will remain secure even if unauthorized parties get access to it.

The art and science of protecting information is now known as "cryptography." The term "cryptography" was formed by fusing two Greek terms, "Krypto" (which means "hidden") and "graphene" (which means writing).

According to historians, cryptography and "normal" writing were born at the same time. As human civilizations progressed, people organized themselves into groups, clans, and kingdoms. These organizations led to the creation of concepts such as wars, powers, sovereignty, and politics. Obviously, these ideas involve information that cannot be shared with ordinary citizens. The group leaders needed to send and receive information through protected means. Thus, cryptography continued to evolve.

The Contributions of Egyptians and Romans

1. Egyptians

The oldest sample of cryptography can be found in Egypt. Ancient Egyptians used hieroglyphs (i.e. a system of writing that involves symbols and images) to share and record pieces of information. In general, these symbols and images are only intelligible to the priests who transmitted messages on behalf of the pharaohs. Here is a sample hieroglyph:

Fig. 1 - Egyptian Hieroglyphs

Several thousands of years later (around 600 to 500 BC), Egyptian scholars started to use simple substitution codes. This style of encoding involved the replacement and/or combination of two or more alphabets using a secret rule. This rule was considered as the "key" in retrieving the real message from the coded "garbage."

2. Romans

Ancient Romans used a system of cryptography known as the Caesar (or Shift) Cipher. This system depends on moving each letter of the message by a certain number (three is the most popular choice). To decode the information, the recipient simply needs to "move" the letters back using the same number. Here is an example:

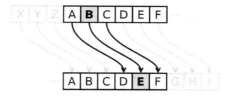

Fig. 2 – Caesar Cipher

Cryptography – Fundamental Concepts

Encryption – This is the process of converting information into an unintelligible form. It helps in securing the privacy of the message while it is being sent to the recipient.

Decryption – This process is the exact opposite of encryption. Here, the encoded message is returned to its natural form.

Important Note: Encryption and decryption requires specific rules in converting the data involved. These rules are known as the key. Sometimes, a single key is used to encrypt and decrypt information. However, there are certain scenarios where these two processes require different sets of keys.

Plaintext and Ciphertext – The term plaintext refers to data that can be read and used without the application of special techniques. Ciphertext, on the other hand, refers to data that cannot be read easily: the recipient needs to use certain decryption processes to get the "real" message.

Authentication – This is probably one of the most important aspects of cryptography. Basically, authentication serves as a proof that the information was sent by the party claimed in the encoded message.]

Let's illustrate this concept using a simple example: John sent a message to Jane. However, before replying, Jane wants to make sure that the message really came from John. This verification procedure can be conducted easily if John does "something" on the message that Jane knows only John can do (e.g. writing his signature, including a secret phrase, folding the letter in a certain way, etc.). Obviously, successful decryption of the message will be useless if the information came from an unwanted source.

Integrity – Loss of integrity is one of the biggest problems faced by people who use cryptography. Basically, loss of integrity occurs whenever the message gets altered while it is being sent to the receiver. Unnecessary and/or unwanted modifications in a message may cause misunderstanding and other issues. Because of this, the message must be protected while it is being delivered. Modern cryptographers accomplish this through the use of a cryptographic hash (i.e. a hash function that is extremely difficult to invert, modify, or recreate).

Non-Repudiation – This concept focuses on ensuring that the sender cannot deny that he/she sent the encoded message. In the example given above, it is important to make sure that John cannot deny the fact that he was the one who sent the message. Modern cryptography prevents this "sender repudiation" using digital signatures.

Chapter 2: The Modern Cryptography

For some people, modern cryptography is the foundation of technology and communications security. This type of cryptography is based on mathematical concepts like the number theory, the probability theory, and the computational-complexity theory. To help you understand modern cryptography, here is a comparison of the "classical" and "modern" types of cryptography.

Classical Cryptography

1. It utilizes common characters (e.g. letters and numbers) directly.

2. It relies heavily on the "obscure is secure" principle. The encryption and decryption processes were considered as confidential information. Only the people involved in the communication can access such data.

3. It needs an entire cryptosystem (will be explained in the next chapter) to complete the "confidential" transfer of information.

Modern Cryptography

1. It relies on modern technology like binary data sequences.

2. The information is encoded through the use of mathematical algorithms accessible to the public. Here, security is achieved through a "secret key" which is used as the foundation for the algorithms. Two factors ensure that "outsiders" cannot access the information even if they have the correct algorithm:

   a. It is extremely difficult to compute such algorithms. Thus, it is hard to extract any information from them.

   b. The absence or presence of secret keys.

3. The encryption doesn't involve the entire cryptosystem. Only the interested parties are required to participate in encoding and decoding the message.

Chapter 3: Cryptosystem – The Basics

A cryptosystem is the application of cryptographic methods and their appropriate coding environment (also called "infrastructure"). This system is used to add security to technology and communications services. Some people refer to cryptosystems as "cipher systems."

To illustrate the concept of cryptosystems, let's consider the following example:

Fig. 3 – A Cryptosystem

In this example, the sender encrypts his message (i.e. the plaintext) through the use of a key. This process converts the plaintext into ciphertext. Once the receiver gets the ciphertext, he uses the same key to decrypt the information. Thus, the ciphertext will be turned into plaintext again.

As you can see, only the parties who have the "key" can access the shared information. Cryptosystems can be divided into these basic components:

- Plaintext – The information that needs to be shared and protected.

- Encryption Algorithm – The mathematical process that uses a plaintext and an encryption key to produce a ciphertext.

- Ciphertext – The coded version of the information. In general, cryptography protects the message itself, not the transmission. That means the coded message is sent through public channels such as emails. Thus, anyone who can access the selected delivery channel can intercept or compromise the message.

- Decryption Algorithm – It is a mathematical process that creates plaintext from any given set of ciphertext and decryption key. Basically, it reverses the encryption process done earlier in the transmission of the message.

- Encryption Key – The value provided by the sender. In creating the ciphertext, the sender enters this key (along with the plaintext) into the encryption algorithm.

- Decryption Key – The value known by the recipient. The decryption key is always related to the encryption key used for the message. However, these keys don't have to be identical. The recipient enters the decryption key and the ciphertext into the decryption algorithm in order to get the plaintext. The collection of all decryption keys for a cryptosystem is known as a "key space."

There are times when an interceptor (also called "attacker") tries to get the encoded message. In general, interceptors are unauthorized entities who want to access the ciphertext and determine the information it contains.

The Two Kinds of Cryptosystems

Currently, cryptosystems are divided into two kinds: (1) Symmetric Key Encryption and (2) Asymmetric Key Encryption. This way of classifying cryptosystems is based on the method of encryption/decryption used for the entire system.

The major difference between the symmetric and asymmetric encryptions is the connection between the encryption and decryption keys. Generally speaking, all cryptosystems involve keys that are closely related. It is impossible to create a decryption key that is totally unrelated to the code's encryption key. Let's discuss each kind of cryptosystems in more detail:

Symmetric Key Encryption

Cryptosystems that belong to this kind have a single key. This key is used to encrypt and decrypt the information being sent. The study of symmetric encryption and systems is known as "symmetric cryptography." Some people refer to symmetric cryptosystems as "secret key" systems. The most popular methods of symmetric key encryption are: IDEA, BLOWFISH, DES (Digital Encryption Standard), and 3DES (Triple-DES).

During the 1960s, 100% of the cryptosystems utilized symmetric encryption. This method of encrypting and decrypting information is so reliable and efficient that it is still being used even today. Businesses that specialize on Communications and Information Technology consider symmetric encryption as the best option available. Since this kind of encryption has distinct advantages over the asymmetric one, it will still be used in the future.

Here are the main characteristics of symmetrically encrypted cryptosystems:

35

- Before transmitting the message, the sender and the receiver must determine the key that will be used.

- The key must be changed regularly to avoid any intrusion into the cryptosystem.

- A stable form of data transmission must be established to facilitate easy sharing of the key between the involved parties. Since the keys must be changed on a regular basis, this mechanism may prove to be expensive and complicated.

- In an organization composed of "x" individuals, to facilitate two-way communication between any two members, the required number of keys for the entire system is derived using the formula: "$x * (x-1)/2$."

- The keys used are often small (i.e. measured through the number of bits involved), so the encryption and decryption processes are faster and simpler compared to those used for asymmetric systems.

- These cryptosystems do not require high processing capabilities from computer systems. Since the keys used are small and simple, ordinary computers can be used to establish and manage the cryptosystem.

Here are the two problems usually encountered when using this kind of cryptosystem:

- Key Determination – Before any message can be transmitted, the sender and the receiver must determine a specific symmetric key. That means a secure and consistent way of creating keys must be established.

- Trust Issues – Because all the people involved use the same key, symmetric key cryptography requires the sender to trust the receiver, and vice versa. For instance, if one of them shares the key with an unauthorized party, the security of the entire cryptosystem will be ruined.

Modern day communicators say that these two concerns are extremely challenging. Nowadays, people are required to exchange valuable data with non-trusted and non-familiar parties (e.g. seller and buyer relationships). Because of these problems, cryptographers had to develop a new encryption scheme: the asymmetric key encryption.

Asymmetric Key Encryption

These cryptosystems use different keys for encrypting and decrypting the message. Although the keys involved are dissimilar, they still have a logical and/or mathematical relationship. It is impossible to extract the message using a decryption key that is totally unrelated to the encryption key.

According to cryptographers, this mode of encryption was developed during the 20th century. It was developed in order to overcome the challenges related to symmetric key cryptosystems. The main characteristics of this encryption scheme are:

- Each member of the cryptosystem should have two different keys – a public key and a private key. When one of these keys is used for encryption, the other one must be used for decryption.

- The private key is considered as confidential information. Each member must protect the private key at all times. The public key, on the other hand, can be shared with anyone. Thus, public keys can be placed in a public repository. As such, some people refer to this scheme as "public key encryption."

- Although the private and public keys are mathematically related, it is practically impossible to determine a key using its "partner."

- When Member1 wants to send information to Member2, he needs to do three things:

  o Obtain Member2's public key from the public repository.

  o Encrypt the message.

  o Transmit the message to Member2. Member2 will acquire the original message using his private key.

- This mode of encryption involves larger and longer keys. That means its encryption and decryption processes are slower compared to those of symmetric encryption.

- The asymmetric key encryption requires high processing power from the computers used in the cryptosystem.

Symmetric key encryption is easy to comprehend. The asymmetric one, however, is quite difficult to understand.

You may be wondering as to how the encryption and decryption keys become related and yet prevent intruders from acquiring a key using its "partner." The answer to this question lies in mathematical principles. Today, cryptographers can create encryption keys based on these principles. Actually, the concept of asymmetric key cryptography is new: system intruders are not yet familiar with how this encryption works.

Here is the main problem associated with asymmetric key cryptosystems:

- Each member needs to trust the cryptosystem. He/she has to believe that the public key used for the transmission is the correct one. That person must convince himself that the keys in the public repository are safe from system intruders.

  To secure the cryptosystem, companies often use a PKI (Public Key Infrastructure) that involves a reputable third party organization. This "outside organization" manages and proves the authenticity of the keys used in the system. The third party company has to protect the public keys and provide the correct ones to authorized cryptosystem members.

Because of the pros and cons of both encryption methods, business organizations combine them to create safer and practical security systems. Most of these businesses are in the communications and information technology industries.

Kerckhoff's Principle

During the 19th century, a Dutch cryptographer named Auguste Kerckhoff identified the requirements of a reliable cryptosystem. He stated that a cryptosystem must be secure even if everything related to it – except the keys – are available to the public. In addition, Mr. Kerckhoff established six principles in designing new cryptosystems. These principles are:

1. The cryptosystem needs to be unbreakable (i.e. in a practical sense). This excludes the system's vulnerability to mathematical intrusions.

2. The system should be secure enough that members can still use it even during an attack from unauthorized entities. The cryptosystem needs to allow authorized members to do what they need to do.

3. The keys used in the system must be easy to change, memorize, and communicate.

4. The resulting ciphertexts must be transmissible by unsecure channels such as telegraph.

5. The documents and devices used in the encryption system must be portable and easy to operate.

6. Lastly, the system must be user-friendly. It should not require high IQ or advanced memorization skills.

Modern cryptographers refer to the second rule as the Kerckhoff principle. They apply it in almost all encryption algorithms (e.g. AES, DES, etc.). Experts in this field consider these algorithms to be completely secure. In addition, these experts believe that the security of the transmitted message relies exclusively on the protection given to the private encryption keys used.

Maintaining the confidentiality of the encryption and decryption algorithms may prove to be a difficult problem. Actually, you can only keep these algorithms secret if you will share them with a few individuals.

Today, cryptography must meet the needs of internet users. Since more and more people gain access to hacking information and advanced computers, keeping an algorithm secret is extremely difficult. That means you should always use the principles given by Kerckhoff in designing your own cryptosystems.

Chapter 4: Different Types of Attacks on Cryptosystems

Nowadays, almost every aspect of human life is affected by information. Thus, it is necessary to safeguard important data from the intrusions of unauthorized parties. These intrusions (also called attacks) are usually classified based on the things done by the intruder. Currently, attacks are classified into two types: passive attacks and active attacks.

Passive Attacks

Passive attacks are designed to establish unauthorized access to certain pieces of information. For instance, activities such as data interception and tapping on a communication channel are considered as passive attacks.

These activities are inherently passive: they do not attempt to modify the message or destroy the channel of communication. They simply want to "steal" (i.e. see) the information being transmitted. Compared to stealing physical items, stealing data allows the legitimate owner (i.e. the receiver) to possess the information after the attack. It is important to note that passive data attacks are more harmful than stealing of physical items, since data theft may be unnoticed by the receiver.

Active Attacks

Active attacks are meant to alter or eliminate the information being sent. Here are some examples:

- Unauthorized modification of the message.

- Triggering unauthorized transmission of data.

- Modification of the data used for authentication purposes (e.g. timestamp, sender's information, etc.).

- Unauthorized removal of information.

- Preventing authorized people from accessing the information. This is known as "denial of service."

Modern cryptography arms people with the tools and methods for preventing the attacks explained above.

The Assumptions of a Cryptosystem Attacker

This section of the book will discuss two important things about system attacks: (1) cryptosystem environments and (2) the attacks used by unauthorized parties to infiltrate cryptosystems.

The Cryptosystem Environment

Before discussing the types of data attacks, it is important to understand the environment of cryptosystems. The intruder's knowledge and assumptions about this factor greatly influence his choices of possible attacks.

In the field of cryptography, three assumptions are made about the attacker and the cryptosystem itself. These assumptions are:

1. Information about the Encryption Method – Cryptosystem developers base their projects on two kinds of algorithms:

    i. Public Algorithms – These algorithms share information with the public.

    ii. Proprietary Algorithms – These algorithms keep the details of the cryptosystem within the organization. Only the users and designers can access information about the algorithm.

    When using a proprietary (or private) algorithm, cryptographers obtain security through obscurity. In general, these are developed by people within the organization and are not thoroughly checked for weaknesses. Thus, private algorithms may have loopholes that intruders can exploit.

    In addition, private algorithms limit the number of people that can join the system. You can't use them for modern communication. You should also remember Kerckoff's principle: "The encryption and decryption keys hold the security of the entire cryptosystem. The algorithms involved can be shared with the public."

    Thus, the first assumption is: "The attacker knows the encryption and decryption algorithms."

2. Obtainability of the Ciphertext – The ciphertext (i.e. the encrypted information) is transmitted through unsecured public channels. Because of this the second assumption is: "The attacker can access ciphertexts created by the cryptosystem."

3. Obtainability of the Ciphertext and the Plaintext – This assumption is more obscure than the previous one. In some situations, the attacker may obtain both the plaintext and the ciphertext. Here are some sample scenarios:

    i.   The attacker convinces the sender to encrypt certain pieces of information and gets the resulting ciphertext.

   ii.   The recipient may share the decrypted information with the attacker. The attacker obtains the corresponding ciphertext from the communication channel used.

  iii.   The attacker may create pairs of plaintexts and ciphertexts using the encryption key. Since the encryption key is in the public domain, potential attackers can access it easily. It's a "hit and miss" type of tactic.

Cryptographic Attacks

Obviously, every attacker wants to break into the cryptosystem and obtain the plaintext. To fulfill this objective, the attacker simply needs to identify the decryption key. Obtaining the algorithms is easy since the information is available publicly.

This means the attacker focuses on obtaining the secret decryption key. Once he/she gets this information, the cryptosystem is broken (or compromised).

Cryptographic attacks are divided into several categories. These are:

- BFA (Brute Force Attack) – Here, the intruder tries to find the decryption key by entering all possible information. For instance, the key contains 8 bits. That means the total number of possible keys is 256 (i.e. 2^8). The attacker tries all of these keys in order to obtain the plaintext. The longer the key, the longer the time needed for successful decryption.

- COA (Ciphertext Only Attack) – This tactic requires the complete set of ciphertexts used for a message. When COA gets the plaintext from the given ciphertexts, the tactic is considered successful. Attackers may also get the corresponding encryption key using this attack.

- CPA (Chosen Plaintext Attack) – This attack requires the attacker to work on the plaintext he/she selected for encryption. Simply put, the attacker has the plaintext-ciphertext combination. It means the task of decrypting the information is easy and simple. It is the first part of the attack – convincing the sender to encrypt certain pieces of information – that presents the most difficulties.

- KPA (Known Plaintext Attack) – With this tactic, the attacker should know some parts of the plaintext. He/she has to use this knowledge to obtain the rest of the message.

- Birthday Attack – This is a subtype of the brute force approach. Attackers use this tactic when working against cryptographic hash functions. Once the intruder finds two inputs that produce similar values, a collision is said to occur: the hash function is broken and the system is breached.

- MIM Attack (Man in the Middle Attack) – This attack is particularly designed for public key cryptosystems. In general, these systems require the exchange of keys before the actual transmission of the ciphertext. Here is an example:

    o Member1 wants to send a message to Member2. To do this, he sends a request for Member2's public key.

    o An intruder blocks the request and sends his own public key.

    o Thus, the unauthorized party acquires the information that will be sent by Member1.

    o To avoid detection, the intruder encrypts the data again and sends it to Member2.

    o The intruder uses his own public key. That means Member2 will see the attacker's key instead of Member1's.

- SCA (Side Channel Attack) – This attack is used to exploit the weaknesses of a cryptosystem's physical implementation. Here, the attackers ignore the system's algorithms and digital protection.

- Fault Analysis Attacks – When using this attack, the intruder looks for errors produced by the system. He/she uses the resulting information to breach the system's defenses.

- Timing Attacks – Here, attackers use the fact that different calculations require different processing times. These people can acquire some data about the message processed by a computer system. They do this by measuring the time used by the computer in performing its calculations.

- Power Analysis Attacks – These attacks are similar to the previous one. However, instead of time, they use the amount of power consumed by the computer system. This information is used to determine the nature of the plaintext.

An Important Note About Cryptographic Attacks

The attacks explained above are theoretical and highly academic. Actually, most of those attacks are defined by cryptography instructors. Some of the attacks you read about involve unrealistic assumptions about the attacker and/or the system's environment.

However, these attacks have excellent potential. Attackers may find ways to improve them. It would be great if you will still consider these attacks when designing your own cryptosystems.

Chapter 5: Traditional Cryptography

You have learned about the basics of modern cryptography. You also discovered the different tools that you can use in designing your own cryptosystems. One of the powerful tools at your disposal is the symmetric key encryption: a mode of encryption that uses a single key for the entire communication process.

This chapter will discuss this mode further so you will know how to apply it in developing cryptosystems.

Old Cryptographic Systems

At this point, you have to study the cryptosystems used in the ancient times. These "old systems" share similar characteristics, which are:

- These cryptosystems are based on the symmetric mode of encryption.

- The message is protected using a single tool: confidentiality.

- These systems use alphabets to facilitate encryption. In contrast, modern cryptosystems use digital data and binary numbers to encrypt a message.

These old systems are called "ciphers." Basically, a cipher is just a group of procedures performed in order to encrypt and decrypt data. You may think of these procedures as the "algorithms" of these ancient cryptosystems.

1. The Caesar Cipher

This cipher is based on a single alphabet. Here, you can create a ciphertext just by replacing every letter of the message with a different one. Cryptologists consider this cipher as the simplest scheme today.

The Caesar Cipher is also called "shift cipher," since each letter is shifted by a fixed number. If you are using the English alphabet, you can use the numbers from 0 to 25. The people involved must choose a certain "shift number" before encoding the plaintext. The number will serve as the encryption and decryption key for the entire communication process.

How to Use the Shift Cipher

1. The sender and the receiver select a shift number.

2. The sender writes down the alphabet twice (i.e. a-z followed by a-z).

3. That person gets the plaintext and finds the appropriate letters. However, he moves the letters based on the shift number selected. For example, if

they are using the number 1, he will replace the letter "A"s with "B"s, the "B"s with "C"s, and so on.

4. The encryption procedure is done once all of the letters have been shifted.

5. The sender transmits the ciphertext to the receiver.

6. The receiver moves the letters of the ciphertext backwards, depending on the shift number being used.

7. Once all of the letters have been shifted, the decryption process is completed. The receiver can use the information he received from the sender.

The Cipher's Security Value

This is not a secure system since the possible encryption keys are extremely limited. If you are using the English alphabet, your possible keys are restricted to 25. This number is not enough for those who need more security. In this situation, an attacker may acquire your key just by carrying out a thorough key search.

2. *The Simple Substitution Cipher*

This is an improved version of the Caesar Cipher. Instead of using numbers to determine the ciphertext, you will choose your own equivalent for each letter of the alphabet. For instance, "A.C... X.Z" and "Z.X... C.A" are two simple permutations of the letters in the English alphabet.

Since this alphabet has 26 letters, the total permutations can be derived through this formula: $4x10^{26}$. The people involved can select any of these permutations to create the ciphertext. The permutation scheme serves as the key for this cryptosystem.

How to Use this Cipher

1. Write down the letters from A to Z.

2. The involved parties choose a permutation for each letter. For example, they might replace the "A"s with "F"s, the "B" with "W", etc. These new letters don't need to have any logical or mathematical relationship with the letter they represent.

3. The sender encrypts the plaintext using the selected permutations.

4. The message is sent to the receiver.

5. The receiver decodes the ciphertext using the chosen permutations.

The Cipher's Security Value

This cipher is way much stronger than the Caesar Cipher. Even strong computer systems cannot decode the ciphertext since the possible permutations (i.e. 4×10^{26}) are too many. Cryptosystems based on this cipher can stop attackers that rely on a brute force approach. However, this substitution system is based on a simple scheme. In fact, attackers have succeeded in breaking letter permutations in the past.

The Monoalphabetic and Polyalphabetic Ciphers

Monoalphabetic Ciphers are ciphers that rely on a single encryption system. In other words, a single encryption alphabet is used for each "normal" alphabet throughout the entire communication process. For instance, if "C" is encoded as "X", "C" must be written as "X" each time it appears in the plaintext.

The two encryption systems discussed above belong to this type.

Polyalphabetic Ciphers, on the other hand, involve multiple encryption alphabets. The encryption alphabets may be switched at different segments of the encryption procedure. Here are two examples of polyalphabetic ciphers:

The Playfair Cipher

This encryption scheme uses pairs of letters to create encryption alphabets. Here, the people involved must create a table where letters are written down. The table used is a 5x5 square (i.e. 25 in total): the squares inside the table hold the letters of the alphabet. Since there are 26 letters in the English alphabet, a letter must be omitted. Cryptographers often omit the letter "J" when using this cipher.

The sender and the receiver must choose a certain keyword, say "lessons." They must write this keyword in the key table, from left to right. In addition, they should not repeat letters. Once the word is written down, the sender/receiver must complete the table using the unused letters (i.e. alphabetically arranged). With the word "lessons" as the keyword and J omitted, the key table should look like this:

L	E	S	O	N
A	B	C	D	F
G	H	I	K	M
P	Q	R	T	U
V	W	X	Y	Z

How to Use this Cipher

1. You should split the message into diagraphs (i.e. pairs of letters). If the total number of letters is an odd number, you should add a Z to the last letter. As an example, let's encrypt the word "human" using the key table created above. It will look like this:

HU MA NZ

2. Here are the encryption rules:

   a. If both letters are in the same column, you should use the letter under each one. You have to go back to the top if you are using the bottom letter. In our example, N and Z are in the same column. Thus, this pair becomes FN.

   b. If both letters are placed in the same row, use the letter located at the right of each one. You need to go back to the first letter of the row if you are working on the rightmost letter. (This rule doesn't apply to our example.)

   c. If none of the previous rules apply, create a rectangle using the pair of letters. Afterward, use the letters on the opposite corner of the correct letters. Work on the letters horizontally. According to this rule, the HU pair is converted to MQ (look at the key table). MA, on the other hand, becomes GF.

3. Using these rules, the word "human" becomes MQ GF FN when encrypted using the Playfair Cipher.

4. You just have to reverse the process if you want to decrypt the message.

The Playfair Cipher's Security Value

This scheme is stronger than the systems discussed earlier. Attackers will have a difficult time analyzing all of the possible keys. In general, cryptologists use this cipher to protect important information. Lots of people rely on the Playfair Cipher since it is easy to use and doesn't require special tools.

The Vigenere Cipher

This encryption scheme uses a word (also known as text string) as the key. This key is used to change the plaintext. For instance, let's use the word "human" as the key. You should convert each letter into its numeric value (i.e. A = 1, B = 2, etc.). In our example:

$$H = 8, U = 21, M = 13, A = 1, N = 14$$

How to Use this Cipher

1. If you want to encrypt "cold water," you have to write the letters down. Then, write the key numbers (i.e. 8, 21, 13, 1, and 14) under the words, one number for each letter. Repeat the numbers as necessary. It looks like this:

C	O	L	D	W	A	T	E	R
8	21	`13	1	14	8	21	13	1

2. Shift the letters of the normal alphabet according to the number written on the table. Here it is:

C	O	L	D	W	A	T	E	R
8	21	13	1	14	8	21	13	1
K	J	Y	E	K	I	O	R	S

3. As you can see, each letter of the plaintext is moved by a different amount – the amount is specified by the key. The letters of your key should be less than or equal to that of your message.

4. To decrypt the message, you just have to use the same key and shift the letters backward.

The Vigenere Cipher's Security Value

This cipher offers excellent security: better than the three ciphers discussed above. Cryptographers use this encryption system to protect military and political data. Because of its apparent invulnerability, security experts call this the "unbreakable cipher."

Chapter 6: Modern Cryptography Schemes

Nowadays, cryptographers use digital data to establish encryption systems. This data is often represented as sets of binary digits (also called "bits"). Modern cryptosystems must process these binary strings to create more strings. Symmetric encryption techniques are categorized based on the procedures performed on the digital information. These categories are:

Block Ciphers

These ciphers group the digital data into separate blocks and process them one at a time. The number of bits contained in a data block is predetermined and unchangeable. Two popular block ciphers, AES and DES, have block sizes of 128 and 64, respectively.

In general, a block cipher uses a set of plaintext data and produces a set of ciphertext data, usually of the same size. Once the block size is assigned, it can no longer be modified. The block size used for the system doesn't affect the strength of encryption techniques involved. The strength of this cipher relies on the length of its key.

Block Size

Although you can use any block size, there are some things you have to consider when working on this aspect of your cryptosystem. These are:

- Avoid small block sizes – Let's assume that a block size is equal to m. Here, the total number of possible plaintext combinations is 2^m. If an intruder acquires the plaintext data used for previous messages, he/she can initiate a "dictionary attack" against your cryptosystem. Dictionary attacks are performed by creating a dictionary of ciphertext and plaintext pairs generated using an encryption key. You should remember this simple rule: the smaller the block size, the weaker the system is against dictionary attacks.

- Don't use extremely large block sizes – Large block sizes mean more processing time for your computer system. Cryptographers working on large bit sizes experience efficiency issues. Often, the plaintext must be padded in order to get the desired block size.

- Use a block size that is a multiple of 8 – Computers can easily handle binary digits that are multiples of 8. You can take advantage of this fact by choosing a block size that has this mathematical property.

Different Types of Block Cipher Schemes

Cryptographers use a variety of block cipher encryption schemes in their systems. Here are some of the most popular block ciphers being used today:

- AES (Advanced Encryption Standard) – This cipher is based on Rijndael, an award-winning encryption algorithm.

- IDEA – This is considered as one of the strongest ciphers available. Its block size is equal to 64 while its key size is equal to 128 bits. Many applications utilize this encryption. For instance, the old versions of PGP (Pretty Good Privacy) protocol used IDEA extensively. Because of patent issues, the utilization of this encryption scheme is restricted.

- DES (Digital Encryption Standard) – This is the most popular block cipher during the 1990s. Because of their small size, DES ciphers are now considered as "broken ciphers."

Stream Ciphers

With this scheme, the information is encrypted one binary digit at a time. The resulting ciphertext is equivalent to the data processed (e.g. 10 bits of plaintext produce 10 bits of ciphertext). Basically, stream ciphers are block ciphers with a block size limit of 1 bit.

Chapter 7: The Pros and Cons of Cryptography

This chapter will discuss the pros and cons of using cryptography.

The Pros

Today, security experts consider cryptography as one of their most useful tools. It provides four things needed for modern communication:

1. Authentication – Cryptographic techniques like digital signatures prevent spoofing and data forgeries.

2. Confidentiality – Encryption schemes protect information from unauthorized parties.

3. Non-repudiation – The digital signatures used in cryptography prove the identity of the sender. Thus, disputes regarding this factor are prevented.

4. Data Integrity – Cryptography involves hash functions that can maintain the integrity of the data being transmitted.

The Cons

Nothing is perfect. Here are the problems associated with cryptography:

- Legitimate users may encounter issues when accessing well-encrypted information. This can turn into a disaster if a certain piece of information has to be obtained quickly.

- Constant availability of information – a basic aspect of communications and information technology – is hard to secure when using cryptography.

- Cryptosystems prevent selective access control. Some organizations need to provide exclusive file access to certain officers. When using cryptosystems, these organizations will have problems in giving selective access to their chosen members. This is because cryptosystems apply the same security measures on every file.

Conclusion

Thank you again for purchasing this book!

I hope this book was able to help you master the basics of cryptography.

The next step is to build your personal cryptosystems so you can easily encrypt messages.

Finally, if you enjoyed this book, please take the time to share your thoughts and post a review on Amazon. It'd be greatly appreciated!

Thank you and good luck!

Book 3
Raspberry Pi 2

By Solis Tech

Raspberry Pi 2 Programming Made Easy!

Raspberry Pi 2: Raspberry Pi 2 Programming Made Easy!

Table of Contents

Introduction

Greetings. Thank you for purchasing this book Raspberry Pi 2: Raspberry Pi 2 Programming Made Easy. If you're reading this book then most likely you are here to learn about his nifty new little computer called the Raspberry Pi. In this book, we'll teach you everything that you need to know to get up and running with this little, but powerful computer.

We'll teach you about its parts, its specifications, setting up the operating system, its capabilities and limitations, and ultimately how to do basic programming. We'll discuss the best programming language that works best with the Raspberry Pi and create your first program with it. Without further ado, let's start your Raspberry Pi journey.

Chapter 1: Raspberry Pi – The Basics

What is a Raspberry Pi?

So what is it exactly? We'll it's a small credit-card sized single board computer that is intended to help people learn more about programming, how the computer works, etc. The CPU or Central Processing Unit is basically a system-on-a-chip. What that means is it pairs an ARM processor that is used by a lot of embedded systems and cellular phones with a Broadcom GPU (Graphics Processing Unit), which is a fairly powerful graphics processor that's capable of displaying full resolution 1080p HD video.

The amount of RAM (Random Access Memory) that the Raspberry Pi 2 has is 1 Gigabyte. Its previous iteration, the Raspberry Pi 1 Model A+ and Raspberry Pi 1 Model B has 256MB and 512MB RAM respectively. The RAM is shared by both the CPU and the GPU.

The Raspberry Pi 2 starts at $39.00 and that includes just the board. On the board there are 4 USB ports, 40 General Purpose Input/Output (GPIO) pins, a full 1080p HDMI port, a Network/Ethernet port, a 3.5mm audio and composite video jack, a Raspberry Pi (CSI) Camera interface, a Video (DSI) Display interface, a Micro SD card slot, and a VideoCore 3D graphics core. The GPIO is basically for more advanced users who are going to be adding Arduino accessory boards, ribbon cables for communication with other hardware devices, and major electronics projects; robotics, sensors, etc.

Why Is it Cool to Have a Raspberry Pi?

Most people think the Raspberry Pi is cool because it's a fairly complete computer, it runs on very little power, it's small, and it will not burn a hole through your wallet; it's $39.00, which is less than the cost that you would pay for a dinner with a friend or a loved one. The Raspberry Pi also helps people that are new to computer hardware get into it and get their hands dirty without the cost and risk associated with more expensive standard hardware.

Another thing that's cool about it is that the Graphics Processing Unit is pretty powerful. It can play 1080p HD video, which makes it really attractive to a lot of people as a Media Center PC. In fact, most people buy the Raspberry Pi 2 for that specific reason because it is a cheap multimedia PC.

What Can You Do With a Raspberry Pi?

So what can you do with this thing? Well, just like what was previously mentioned, if you're really new to computer hardware, the Pi can help you learn about those individual components of most modern computers. And if you want to learn how to do programming, the Raspbian operating system that comes with the Raspberry Pi 2 comes with a lot of tools for programming to help you get started.

So you might be asking, why wouldn't you start learning how to program with the computer that you already have? Well, you can. And that's perfectly fine. However, you can think of the Raspberry Pi as your little playground and your test computer that you don't have to worry about breaking if you screw something up. Even if you do break it, you'll only be losing $39.00.

But if you don't care about all that and you don't care about programming or about learning the hardware and so forth, the Raspberry Pi 2 also makes a really great little Media PC. You can get a small case for it, hook it up to the network, install another operating system that's based on Linux called OpenELEC, which is basically a back-end for XBMC (Xbox Media Center), plug it into your TV, and you're ready to start streaming video and audio content on your high-definition TV.

Chapter 2: Hardware Accessories

In this chapter, we're going to talk about some of the hardware and accessories that you're going to need to get started with the Raspberry Pi 2. First, let's start out with the bare necessities. The two things that you'll definitely need are power and an SD card.

Power Requirement

Let's take a moment here and talk about power because it's important. The Raspberry Pi is a little picky about its power source. Learning about what you need here for power could save you a lot of headache later down the road. The Raspberry Pi needs 5 volts. That should be anywhere between 4.75 volts minimum and a maximum of 5.25 volts. It should be at least 700 mAh, but the recommended is 1000 mAh.

The reason for the 1000 mAh recommended power is because when you start plugging in a keyboard, mouse, network cable, and other peripherals, these all pull power away from the system. This is also why some Raspberry Pi 2 users say that 1500 mAh to 2000 mAh is even better. Of course, if you're only doing projects close to your desktop computer and you don't really plan to run the Raspberry Pi 24/7, you could just run it off of your desktop system's power with just a USB cable if you want.

SD Card Storage

There is not on-board storage on the Raspberry Pi. So you need an SD card to run the operating system from and also to store any files. Get at least the Class 4 SD storage. It is recommended that you get the Class 6 or Class 10 if you don't mind spending a little bit more.

However, if it's not available, just get the best one that you can. The cost difference honestly isn't that much, and SD cards are getting cheaper all the time. You'll also need a card reader to transfer the operating system image that you're going to download off of Raspberry Pi's website from your desktop computer to the SD card. You can also buy SD cards with the operating system pre-installed from whosoever your Raspberry Pi vendor is if ever you want to skip the operating system installation on the Pi.

If you want to try out multiple operating systems, you can do that with a single card. However, just keep in mind that you'll overwrite any of your settings that you've played around with in the operating system.

Interacting With the Raspberry Pi

You'll need to decide on how you want to interact with your Raspberry Pi. You can either do it headless over a network, with a keyboard, mouse and monitor, or you can do a combination of both. For network access, you're going to need a network cable; either a CAT5e or CAT6 to connect to your router. There's also a USB WiFi option, which allows you to connect to your router wirelessly.

If you're going headless, you don't really need a USB keyboard and mouse. They are both optional. It just depends on what you want to use the Raspberry Pi for. Just like what was previously mentioned, if you don't want to use the desktop interface, you can skip using a mouse and just plug in a keyboard. If you're using it as a media center and navigate XBMC, a wireless Bluetooth keyboard is a fantastic option if you want to sit on your couch and navigate your media center.

If you're only planning to login remotely using SSH, you can skip the keyboard entirely, or if you want you can just borrow a keyboard and mouse from another machine for the initial setup before you actually go headless over the network. Raspberry Pi should automatically get an IP address from your router. After your router gives an IP address to your Pi, you can just log in to your router to see the exact IP address that was assigned. You can then connect via SSH using that IP address.

If you don't want to find out what the exact IP address is via the router and instead want to find it out locally, you can pull up the command terminal in Raspbian OS and execute an "ifconfig" command. You can then unplugged your peripherals and go headless from there.

Displays

Moving on to displays, if your TV or monitor has an HDMI input, that's great because all you'll need to get is a cheap HDMI cable. If your monitor only has DVI-in, you'll need an HDMI to DVI cable or an adapter. Just keep in mind that if you do that, the audio signal that's coming out of the HDMI port will be ignored when you're using a DVI converter.

Depending on your setup, you can use external speakers or a splitter. If you're going to go headless, you can skip purchasing a separate monitor specifically for your Pi and just borrow one for the initial setup if you want to. Otherwise, you can still do most of the setup across the network if you are connected via SSH.

Raspberry Pi Casing

Moving forward, even though it may look cool keeping your bare board out with a bunch of wires just hanging off, it is probably not the safest thing to do for your Raspberry Pi. So it is recommended that you get a case for your Pi. You can get a prefab case for as little as $5.00. It is completely optional but it does help protect the board. A number of people have made some pretty cool custom cases, all of which are available for purchase on-line.

Chapter 3: Installing the Operating System In Your SD Card

In this chapter we're going to be looking at operating system options and how to actually install it in your Raspberry Pi. First off, you're going to need to consider what your goal is for your Raspberry Pi. Is this going to be a learning or tinkering board? Are you going to be programming or do you just want a quick and cheap home theater PC? For a more general purpose operating system or for the tinkerer and programmer, most people recommend going for Raspbian OS.

The latest version of Raspbian at the time of this writing is Raspbian Jessie Kernel Version 4.1, which was released in November 2015. For a home theater PC, most people recommend getting either OpenELEC or RaspBMC. If you're just not sure and you want to try multiple operating system versions, get two or three SD cards and you can just install a different operating system on each of them. You can swap them out depending on what you feel like doing with your Raspberry Pi. Below is the link where you can download the various operating systems for your Pi:

https://www.raspberrypi.org/downloads/

The Operating system installation method that we're about to discuss is mainly for those who have a Mac or a Linux desktop. If you have Windows, the concept is still pretty much the same. You'll just use a different program to get the disk image onto your SD card with Windows.

Step 1

Regardless of which type of PC you're using, you're going to need to download the disk image or images of your preferred operating system for your Raspberry Pi. These are by no means the only options, just the ones that the Raspberry Pi community recommends in order to get you started. The first one, as we've mentioned before, is Raspbian.

There's also another version that came out called Occidentalis, which is actually based on Raspbian but has a more educational slant to it and includes a lot more educational tools. For a home theater PC, you'll want to install either OpenELEC or RaspBMC. Both of these are built around the XBMC (Xbox Media Center).

Step 2

Once you have chosen your operating system, click the download link and choose a location in your computer that you're going to easily remember. Once your download is complete, it would probably be in a .zip file format so you'll need to unzip it and you should now have an image file with an .img file extension. There are a lot of different methods to get this image onto the SD card, but if you're on Linux or Mac, we're just going to use the "dd" command to write the image on the card.

We're going with this method mainly because it's installed in almost every UNIX-based system and it should work pretty much the same on all of them. Before we proceed in talking about DD in Mac or Linux, if you're a Windows PC user, you're going to need to download the win32 disc imager. Once you've installed it, you need to run it and tell it where the operating system image file is located on your hard drive and what drive letter to write the image to for your SD card.

When choosing the actual drive letter that points to your SD card, make sure that the SD card you're using is blank since everything inside it is going to be overwritten. Getting back to Linux and Mac, you want to open up a new shell or a terminal as it's called on the Mac, and then navigate to the folder where you downloaded your disk image. In most cases it would be in /Downloads/Raspberry Pi/Raspbian.

Again, keep in mind that you will be overwriting everything on the SD card that you're going to be using for this installation. So use a fresh card or one you don't mind overwriting. At this point, make sure you do not have your SD card reader plugged in yet. The reason for this is because we need to find out which device our SD card will be using.

In your terminal or shell, type "df" (without the quotes) and then press ENTER. Now you should see a list of devices and the folders where they are mounted. This should be any of your internal hard drives or external hard drives and so forth. Now is the time when you want to plug in your SD card into your reader and then plug the reader into an open USB port.

Just wait a few moments for the card to mount. This can take a few seconds. After a few seconds, use the "df" command again. You should now see something different; an item that's listed as either no-name or volume/untitled. On the side you should see something listed like dev/disk3s1 or on Linux it would be something similar to dev/sdb1 or sdc1 or something like that next to it.

Drive assignments may vary from user to user so just take which device is listed next to that volume carefully. You want to make sure that you're using the SD device and not one of your hard drives. DD is an unforgiving command and it will overwrite without prejudice and without asking you if you're sure about doing so. So just be very careful. We can't stress this enough. You don't want to overwrite your main hard drive.

Once you know the device that you're going to write to, remember or write it down. Like what we mentioned earlier, it should be something like dev/disk3s1 on a Mac or something similar to dev/sdc1 on Linux. We're going to change this a little bit since we actually want to write the disk image to the entire card not just a partition on the card, which is what we have mounted right now.

So what we need to do now is unmount the SD card's partition before we can write to the entire card. We don't want to eject the card, we just want to unmount it. On your Mac you can open up your Disk Utility. It's in the same folder as your terminal. You then have to select the volume under the SD card device and click "unmount." You can also do this from the terminal, but you'll need to be on the superuser account. So to use Disk Utility using a superuser or root account, you can type the command below:

    $ sudo diskutil unmount/dev/disk3s1

On Linux you would do a similar thing. You would type in the command below:

    $ sudo unmount /dev/sdc1

You can type the command above or whatever your device assignment happens to be. One thing to remember is that the sudo command will always ask you for the administrator password in order to be able to execute the command, regardless of whether you're using a Mac or a Linux system. Once the SD card's partition is unmounted, we're going to run DD with 3 arguments; "bs," "if," and "of." Those stand for block size, in file, and out file respectively. You'll run the command exactly as below:

```
$ dd bs=1m if=2015-12-24-jessy-raspbian.img of=/dev/sdc1
```

Looking at the command above, you're going to be putting a value for block size; specifically 1m which stands for 1 megabyte, for "if" you'll be putting the name of the image file, and "of" is the location where you stored the image file. Regarding the location of the image file, we're going to change that a little bit. For example, if your device is listed as /dev/disc3s1, you want to change the "of" argument to /dev/rdisk3s1.

This may be different depending on your system so changing this will make sure that you use the entire SD card and not just the partition. In Linux for example, the "of" value would probably be something like /dev/sdb1 or /dev/sdc1. In this case, the letter after the letters "sd" could be different depending on your system. So in order to write to the whole card, you just need to take away the number "1." You should have something similar to the one below:

```
$ dd bs=1m if=2015-12-24-jessy-raspbian.img of=/dev/sdb
```

So that's pretty much of it. Once you're confident that you have the correct arguments for the DD command, hit ENTER. You're going to wait a few minutes while the SD card is being written on. At this point, you won't see any output while this process is ongoing. It will probably take a few minutes so just be patient.

If you're on Linux and you get an error, you might need to change the "bs" value from 1m to 1M (capital M). For some reason the case of the letter matters to a Linux system. Once this has been completed, you should be back to a command prompt. And assuming everything worked properly, you will now have a bootable operating system on your SD card.

You are now ready to boot your Raspberry Pi for the first time and start configuring your system, which we will cover on the next chapter.

Chapter 4: Booting OpenELEC & Raspbian for the First Time On Your Pi

In the last chapter, we installed the operating system on the SD card. Let's now go ahead and insert the SD card into the slot on the underside of the Raspberry Pi. Keep in mind that the metal contacts of the SD card should be facing the underside of the board. First, we'll need at least a keyboard, a mouse, and a monitor. Go ahead and plug the keyboard and mouse to any of the available USB ports. Second, go ahead and plug in the Ethernet CAT5 or CAT6 cable on the Ethernet port on the Pi. Make sure that the other end of the Ethernet cable is plugged into your router. Third, go ahead and plug in the HDMI cable for your monitor.

Do not forget to use an HDMI to DVI converter if you have a DVI monitor. Lastly, plug in the microUSB cable of the 5V power supply to the microUSB port on your Raspberry Pi. Once you have everything plugged in, you should see the LEDs on the board start to light up. You will also see that the boot cycle has now started on the monitor. Just wait for login prompt to appear once the boot process has finished.

Logging In

Once you have the login prompt, you want to use the default username which is "pi", and the default password, which is "raspberry" in all lower case. Once you type those in and press ENTER, you're in.

To start the desktop interface just type "start x" and press ENTER. Most people should be pretty familiar with how this desktop works. It's very similar to most other modern GUI interfaces. Let's now take a look at some of the applications that are available to you once you've successfully started the desktop interface of your Raspberry Pi.

- Scratch – This is basically a programming teaching tool. It is very similar to Karel. If you've ever taken a programming class, they use Karel the robot to teach you basic programming concepts.

- Python – Python is basically a very versatile and robust programming

69

language. It is used by many programmers and companies to make web based applications.

- Midori – Midori is a lightweight web browser. It takes its roots from Mozilla Firefox.

- File Manager – The file manager is very similar to the Window file manager. It lets you see the different directories and storage media that's associated with your Raspberry Pi. It also lets you see the important files in your Raspberry Pi.

- Terminal – Since Raspbian is basically a derivative of Debian Linux, it's no surprise that it also has a terminal similar to Linux. It has the same functions as a Linux terminal. It can also run all the terminal commands that you can run in a Linux system.

Now that we've pretty much seen what the Raspbian operating system looks like, let's go on ahead and see what OpenELEC looks like in a Raspberry Pi. Go ahead and mount the image of OpenELEC onto your SD card. The mounting process for OpenELEC is pretty much the same as Raspbian. If you're still logged into Raspbian on your Raspberry Pi, you must log out and shut the Pi down.

You shut the Raspberry Pi down by using the "halt" command. Again, in order for this command to work, you have to be a superuser. So you need to type in the word "sudo," then put a space by pressing the spacebar, type in the word "halt," and then press ENTER.

After you press ENTER, the Raspberry Pi will initiate the shutdown process. Once finished, you can now switch to the SD card with the OpenELEC operating system. Once the card is inserted, you can start booting your Raspberry Pi with the OpenELEC operating system. As you can see, you can pretty quickly change out cards and be up and running with a different operating system pretty quickly.

Once you have OpenELEC up and running, go ahead and explore the different parts of the operating system, see the different programs it has, and find out what it can do. This is the perfect time to explore and learn what the Raspberry Pi and its operating system is all about.

Chapter 5: How to Get Around in the Raspberry Pi's Unix-based Command Line Interface

In this chapter, we will be going through some of the more basic commands that you're going to need to know in the command line shell for getting around the Unix-based file system. If you're running Raspbian, you'll need to know some of the standard Unix commands. Like most systems in Linux or Unix, files are stored in directory hierarchies.

You can also call them folders if you want to feel more comfortable with that term. When you login, unless you have a custom setting, you will most likely begin in your home/username directory. For Raspbian, the default username that we've been logging in with is Pi. So your home directory is going to be /home/Pi.

Most users on the system, except for root, will have their home directory stored within /home. The main exception is the root user's folder, which is stored in /root. On your command prompt you will see your home directory represented as a tilde symbol "~", and you can use that to easily get back to your home folder anytime.

Moving forward, let's get into working with directories. The first thing you might want to know is where you are and what directory you are located in. The first command that we're going to start with is PWD. PWD stands for Print Working Directory, which tells you the current directory that you're located in at that moment. You'll find that most commands in Unix are abbreviations of the activity that they perform.

As you can see from the output after you typed in PWD and pressed ENTER, you're in /home/pi. If you want to change to another directory, you need to use the CD command. For example, if you want to go to the top level directory—also called the root, which is not to be confused with the root user home directory—you type in this command:

$ cd /

71

cd / represents the main directory; and the slash that is used is a forward slash. Many people mistakenly use the term backslash when they really mean forward slash. We call the "/" a forward slash because we read from left to right. So a slash leaning to the right is in the forward direction.

Typing the aforementioned command and pressing ENTER will bring you to the top level directory. There is nothing above this top level directory. It only has subdirectories beneath it. With that being said, let's now take a moment to look at a few subdirectories beneath the main root directory.

The first one that we're going to look at is "etc." Etc stores many of the system's configuration files so get familiar with this folder. If you want to change configuration settings, you're going to come here often. To go to the etc subdirectory from the root directory, type in the command below:

$ cd /etc

Now let's take a look at what's inside etc. We do that using the "ls" command. Ls is short for list and it just lists directory contents. ls also have some options associated with it that allows the user to change the way the listing looks.

Let's go ahead and take a look at a few common options of ls:

- -a – lists all files including hidden files in the directory. Files beginning with a dot "." are considered hidden. So anything that you name with a dot preceding the file name will be hidden automatically, unless you use the -a option to list the files.

- -l – lists all the files lengthwise down the screen.

- -p – puts a forward slash after the directory, which is inside the current directory that you are viewing. This lets you easily distinguish directories from files.

- --color – this will give you a colorful directory listing. However, this doesn't always work. This command works depending on the system and if you're logging in remotely.

You can also combine multiple options with a single dash. Look at the example below:

$ ls -lap

Typing the command above will give you all the options that you've indicated together with the list command. Now, to go back a directory, you have two options. In this particular case we can either type cd / to take us back to the main root directory since that's where we started before going into etc, or we can type the command below:

$ cd ..

That's "cd" followed by a space, and then two dots. This takes us back one directory. We also have another command below:

$ cd ../..

This command takes us back two directories if you happen to be two subdirectories in. So if you're still in the "etc" directory, go back one directory. There are a number of other directories to familiarize with within the root directory. Below are some of those directories:

- /bin – this directory is for commands and binaries.

- /sbin – this is for system and administrator commands.

- /user – this is for user-related files. It also has its own /bin and /sbin subdirectories.

- /var – var stands for variable. The /var/log subdirectory is a common destination for users who troubleshoot problems whose log file end up here.

- /home – As what we discussed before, this is for the user directories.

- /mnt – mnt, which stands for Mount, is pretty much the mount point for any external drives, image files, or things like that.

- /dev – this is for devices that interface with the hardware.

- /lib – this is for programs and program libraries.

There a lot more, but this is just a quick rundown of the more common directories that you're likely to encounter and use.

So how do we add, remove, or modify files and directories? Well, to create a new directory, type in the command below:

$ mkdir directoryname

Mkdir stands for make directory. This should be followed by a space and then the name of the directory that you want to create. To remove that empty directory, just used the command below:

$ rmdir directoryname

Rmdir stands for remove directory. This should be also followed by a space and then the name of the directory that you want to remove. Keep in mind that using this command with a non-empty directory would result to an error. There's another option to remove a directory even though it contains files and subdirectories. However, it can be a little dangerous in the wrong hands if they don't know what they're doing.

So please use with caution whenever you utilize the below command:

```
$ rm -rf directoryname
```

The -r option after the remove command means to do the removing process recursively, which drills down into the subdirectories located within the directory you're trying to remove. The -f option stands for Force, which forces the process to go through. So executing this command basically tells the system that you know what you're doing.

The system will allow you to execute the command as long as you have permission to that file or directory. Again, use these options only if you really need to. There won't be any dialogue box, pop-up window, or anything like that to save you from making a mistake with this command.

For copying files and directories, you'll be using the CP command. Look at the example command below:

```
$ cp filename1 filename2
```

First type in the cp command, followed by a space, followed by the name of the file to copy from, followed by another space, and then lastly the name of the file to copy to. Note that filename 1 and filename 2 should be different. Also, keep in mind that you need to have root (sudo) access in order to successfully execute this file.

To rename or move a file without duplicating it, use the command below:

```
$ mv filename1 filename2
```

The above command will essentially move the contents of filename1 to filename2. You can also specify directories where files are located. For example, let's say you want to copy the contents of /etc/hosts to your home folder. For that you would use the below command:

$ cp /etc/hosts /home/pi

Type in the cp command, followed by a space, then followed by the file-path of the file that you want to copy, and then another space, and then followed lastly by the file-path of the location where you want to copy the file to.

To move or copy a directory and its subdirectories, you want to use the -r option, which is again a recursive option.

$ cp -r directory1 directory2

If you want to find out about any of these commands, you can use the MAN command. MAN stands for manual. If you want to find out more about the cp command for example, you just have to type the command below:

$ man cp

This will pull up all the information about the cp command and all the options associated with it. The same applies to the mv, rm, and so forth.

Chapter 6: Python Programming in Raspberry Pi

In this chapter, we're going to look at the best programming language for the Raspberry Pi; Python. It is considered by many as a notably powerful and dynamic language that is used to develop numerous application domains. Most programmers compare Python to Perl, Java, Ruby, Tcl, or Scheme. This is why Python is the primary language the Raspberry Pi is designed to operate on.

Below are some of the key features of the Python programming language:

- Superb for programming veterans and also remain simple enough for beginners to understand.

- Excellent scalability. Python is excellent in small projects; even better for large scale ones.

- Extremely portable and is compatible across all platforms

- Hardware embeddable

- Elegant and simple to understand syntax and semantics

- Excellent stability

- Has a huge standard library of pre-built subroutines, codes, etc.

Moving forward, we'll discuss how to get a very simple python program working. In addition, we'll also discuss how to use the Graphical User Interface to code basic python programs. However, what this chapter won't tackle is the nitty-gritty of learning how to program in Python. Python object-oriented programming is a whole topic in itself and is therefore out of the scope of this book.

Python programming in the Raspberry Pi is similar to Python programming using a normal desktop or laptop computer. It's just that with the Raspberry Pi, you're programming in a very portable, cheap, but robust platform. To start programming with Python on your Raspberry Pi, you must first make sure that you've successfully installed the Raspbian operating system.

Using the desktop of your Raspbian OS, click on the Menu option on the taskbar. Clicking on menu allows you to see the sub-menus for Raspbian. Click on the "Programming" sub-menu. Once you do that, you'll be presented with different programming applications for Raspbian. One of those applications would be your Python Editor.

Python Editors vary depending on the version of Raspbian running in your Raspberry Pi. However, the most common Python IDE would be Stan's Python Editor or SPE. Click on that and you'll be presented with GUI (Graphical User Interface) for your Python IDE (Integrated Development Environment).

The main window of your Python IDE is where you'll type the source code of the program that you're developing. To start making our simple Python program, first create a folder on your Raspbian desktop where we will put our python script. Just right click on any empty space on your desktop and click "Create New Folder." Don't forget to give your new folder a name.

Now, let's go ahead and develop a simple "Hello World" program using Python. To do so, go to   the code editor window of your Python IDE and type in the following code:

```
1      print "Hello World"
```

After typing this code in your editor, save it by clicking on the "File" menu at the menu of your Python IDE and then click on "Save." You will have to give your python script a name. In this case, just type in the filename as HelloWorld.py and save it inside the new folder that you have created on your desktop. Take note that filenames should not contain any spaces and that it should have a .py extension. This is the file extension for all Python scripts.

After saving the file, run the program by clicking on the "run" button on the menu bar of your Python IDE. At this point, two things should happen depending on which Python IDE you're using. Some IDEs will pull up the terminal and display the output of the program from there, while other IDEs will have a status bar at the bottom where it will show you the output of the Python program that you just ran.

Regardless of whatever mode of output your IDE uses, it should display the words "Hello World." If you want to run your Python script from the terminal itself and not from the IDE, all you need to do is navigate to where your Python script is located first and run the script from there. To do this, type the command below:

$ cd /home/pi/Desktop/foldername

The "foldername" is the name of the folder that you have created on the desktop. Once you're there type the below command to display the contents of that folder:

$ ls -l

Now, you'll see your HelloWorld.py file. To run this just type in the below command:

$ python HelloWorld.py

The command above is basically telling the system to use the Python interpreter to open the HelloWorld.py file. Press ENTER and you'll see the output; "Hello World."

Congratulations, you've just made your first Python program in your Raspberry Pi.

Conclusion

Thank you for purchasing and reading this book. We hope that we've taught you all the basic things that you need to know about your Raspberry Pi; how to set it up, how to install the operating system so that you'll be able to develop programs using it.

From here, developing more intricate programs using Python is just a matter of learning the nitty-gritty of the programming language itself. There are many online tutorials out there that you can go and see to get in-depth knowledge of Python programming. Python is a very versatile and stable programming language and using it to make your Pi do wondrous things is easy, as long as you have an advanced knowledge of the programming language itself.

Again, Thank you so much and we hope that you succeed in your quest for knowledge on the Python programming language and that you have fun in finding ingenious ways to use your Raspberry Pi.